The Lonely Heart

A Guide to Living a Successful Single Life

Tiffany Watkins

ISBN: 0615639305
ISBN-13: 9780615639307

Dedication

This book is first dedicated to the Creator of Heaven and earth, my Lord and savior Jesus Christ. God without you I could not have walked this single walk that I have. Although I have fallen and made many mistakes throughout my singleness, you were there to pick me up. God you are my husband first and my life-line. I love you with all of my heart. Thank you for being the shoulder I cried on in my bed during those many lonely nights. You were always there to strengthen me in prayer when I thought I would lose my mind and wanted to give up. Your supernatural power gave me the strength to continue to press on. Thank you for sending your angels and a tangible reminder that you are always with me. ☺

Secondly, this book is also dedicated to my Archbishop Harris E. Clark, who has been and continues to be a listening ear and support to me as I continue to grow in ministry. Thank you for supporting me when others wouldn't. Thank you for encouraging me when others couldn't and thank you for just being you. You are truly the spiritual father that I asked God for. I am glad God sent you to be a part of this major transition and elevation in my life. Every time I think about God sending you into my life, I am truly amazed by his love for me. Words could never express my gratitude for the love you have shown as a father. You have truly allowed God to shine through you to push me to where I need to be in him. I will always thank him for sending you and Elect-Lady Betty Clark into my life. Lady Clark I truly enjoy those personal talks we share when I can let my hair down, especially during our trip to Chicago. You always know how to make me laugh! I love both of you to life!

Last but certainly not least, I want to dedicate this book to my spiritual mother. Thank you for being the loving and giving person you are. I will always cherish and never forget you. Your mentorship and life coaching class has been invaluable in my life and has truly propelled me into the woman I have become and continue to become in ministry. Thank you for encouraging me to begin again in 2010; to transition toward my freedom and to move into my real destiny! I truly meant what I said when I told you that it was watching your preaching after my pastor's death that kept my spirit alive. It doesn't matter when, I can always pick up a DVD of yours when I am down and it jolts my spirit back to where I need to be. As I said before…I will be one of the best mentee's you have ever had!!!

Special Thanks

First I want to thank my mother and father who gave me breath. Thank you for always loving me and being in my life.

To my sister Elder Felicia Brownlee, thank you for standing by me in the hard times with your love, support, and encouragement. You could have desired to no longer stand with me after that "combat boot situation" we experienced as little children, but you stuck with me through the thick and the thin and I love you for that! (Smile)

I also want to thank my friend Trinita Chapple who has worked with me to proofread and edit this book. I am looking forward to the great things that God has promised in your life. I love you and you are much appreciated.

To my friend Pastor Natasha Lee who has helped me in so many ways during my first year of trusting the Lord in full time ministry. I am glad for the divine connection that God brought between us during the life coach class.

Thank you for your support, words of encouragement, and motivation as I stepped out in faith!

Special thanks to Overseer Lawan Neely for your giving and loving heart.

Special thanks also to Pastor/Prophet Robert Anorchie. Thank you for your personal prophetic prayers and your prophetic prayer line. Your prophetic words of encouragement have proven to be invaluable in my life.

Finally, to my Renewed Faith Ministries church family, thank you for your love, support, time and investment in your pastor. You all are truly loved and appreciated! I couldn't ask for a better church family!!!

Endorsements

It has been one of my greatest privileges to know and walk with Pastor Tiffany Watkins over the past four years. Her ministry and teachings come from the trenches of her experiences. This book is more than just another good manual on singleness; you have in your hands a stick of dynamite loaded with spiritual power and impartation that comes from one of the modern-day Apostles' who has walked what she talks. Your hunger for God will grow and your appetite for this world will diminish when you devour this book. This book has been given to her by God to let us know that in your singleness you can have and live a victorious life with Christ.

Archbishop Harris E. Clark
Kingdom Vision Worship Center
Starr, South Carolina

As a happily married wife and mother, I would personally recommend this book to all singles, married, those thinking about marriage, those not thinking about marriage, or divorced. This book reaches all genres of people. She deals with core issues that are helpful not only for singles but for those who are married. The book addresses the "nitty gritty" issues when talking with potential mates. I believe the book would help a lot of marital issues and would deter a lot of potential divorces for singles looking to get married. She shares important keys on how to understand the way men and woman think through different opinions. She also addresses many issues preachers often shy away from in the pulpit. It would be my hope that one day there would be many seminars to follow. It reaches down to the core when dealing with sex, loneliness, and relationships. I would recommend this book be taught to many church singles groups. This book is a must have for your personal library.

Elder Felicia Brownlee
Anderson, South Carolina

Pastor Watkins, this is a most powerful and dynamic book! Thank you so much for not being afraid to share from your past hurts and what many would dare to call "mess".... I believe that this book exemplifies the truth found in the statement "God will take our mess and turn it into our ministry." The things that you not only encountered, but also endured, will definitely be an example to many that Gods' blood is all powerful and He can do anything but fail!

This book will definitely be a deliverance tool for many and will open the eyes of those who are saved, lost, and anyone in between - it will even help those of us who claim salvation, but continue to live in sin. I pray that as each person reads this book, they will be open to the Spirit of God and allow Him to bring total healing and deliverance to their lives in order that they may be propelled into a POWERFULLY DYNAMIC FUTURE - just like you! God bless you for not being afraid to share where you were and what you did to overcome. Thank you for being a vessel used by God....

Trinita King-Chapple
Baltimore, Maryland

Finally it's here! This is a book that deals with real issues in a tangible way. Pastor Watkins has taken on many issues in this book that we deal with in relation to others and in relation to ourselves. She has, through the Spirit, revealed not just what we deal with but why we wrestle with some areas and have revealed the keys to cause us to conquer. Pastor Watkins provides a road map to take you through healing and into your divine destiny; journey with her through each chapter as you gain insight, deliverance, and power.

Pastor Natasha Lee
Gainesville, Florida

Table of Contents

Guarding the Heart While Waiting on God

Introduction

I can remember this day vividly, it was one day in January at 8:34 p.m. I remember being surrounded with children and still feeling very much alone. I would often have children to surround me in order to help cheer me up whenever I would feel down. However, on this particular day, no matter how much I played with the children, I continued to draw deeper and deeper into a state of somber. I remember trying to text a couple of my friends only to find that they weren't free to talk at the time. I was at a point where I longed to have a physical touch to drain my somber heart; yet I was faced with the realization that the touch I desired to have was not there. I could feel myself slipping into a state of somberness and desolation. I couldn't understand what was going on because I was finally starting to be at a place where things were looking up for me in my life, but I still couldn't shake the loneliness I felt at that moment. It was as if I was being pulled further and further into a zombie state. Although people were talking around me, it was as if the voices I heard were hollow echoes of endless babble that melted in one ear and out the other. My soul had drifted into a morbid place of emptiness in a matter of minutes. On the outside I was talking and laughing with the family and children but on the inside I was drifting into an endless sea of solitude.

I would venture to say that there are many people who end up at this place and don't understand why. If you are reading this book, nine times out of ten you have been there at least once in your lifetime. For some, things may be looking good on the outside of your life but there still continues to be a nagging void that is unable to be filled. For others, nothing in your life is going right and you become more and more lonely and depressed every day. I often hear married people say that even though they love their mates dearly, there still seems to be a longing in their lives. Some of you reading this book may not be single but married and you have a mate that is abusing you or cheating on you. Although you know he is abusing you or cheating on you, you still choose to stay for fear of loneliness.

How do we get rid of this deep void of loneliness? How can we live productive lives and resist the pull to be drawn into the cave of loneliness? In this book, I will begin to discuss the pitfalls of falling into this place of loneliness and how to counteract it. I will also deal with every day singles and singles in ministry living a successful single life while escaping the pitfalls of loneliness and other temptations.

Chapter 1

The Lonely Heart

The heart is a unique organ because without it one cannot live. The heart pumps blood to other vital organs in the body. It is also the seat of your emotions and a place where the spirit of God can flow. Proverbs 4:23 tells us to *"Keep thy heart with all diligence; for out of it are the issues of life."* What issues in your heart have you not kept with all diligence? What have you allowed to come in and affect you so that you are left empty, void, and lonely? These questions and many more have to be asked and answered before you can move out of the state of loneliness and into a life of fulfillment.

I want to explain the definition for loneliness. According to the Merriam-Webster dictionary, to be lonely means to "lack companionship, to be separated from or unfrequented by others." Loneliness is also "having a feeling of depression or sadness resulting from the consciousness of being alone." (Merriam-Webster Dictionary)

We have to recognize that even if the whole world is against us, God is for us. Once we can rest in this truth we will be comfortable in knowing that God is always with us. I can remember one morning in March the enemy was really laying heavy on me. That morning I felt so alone. I felt like Elijah when he ran away from Jezebel. He had been obedient to God and defeated the prophets of Baal but Jezebel was now seeking to kill him. Elijah was in a morbidly lonely place.

We can see this in 1 Kings 19:9-10 where Elijah hid in a cave. It says, "*And he came thither unto a cave, and lodged there; and, behold, the word of the LORD came to him, and he said unto him, What doest thou here, Elijah? And he said, I have been very jealous for the LORD God of hosts: for the children of Israel have forsaken thy covenant, thrown down thine altars, and slain thy prophets with the sword; and I, **even I only, am left**; and they seek my life, to take it away.*" Elijah said "even I only am left." He felt like there was no one with him and that he was all alone.

During a period of about seven years of my life, this was how I felt. I was in a place where I had lost my pastor, who was also my spiritual mother. She was not only my spiritual mother, but my sister and mentor. I can remember traveling in ministry and enjoying life; they were the best years of my life until tragedy struck when she was diagnosed with cancer and died. There were many people that thought that I wouldn't make it, but I did because I was determined to serve God. Although I loved my spiritual mom I loved God more. Therefore, I couldn't give up! She had introduced the importance of a relationship with God to me so now I had to stand on him alone.

I was licensed as a minister four months later and five years later I was ordained as the Pastor of the same ministry that my spiritual mother led. The Overseer of the church passed away a couple of years later and many things started to happen that constantly pushed me into a place of loneliness.

When I became a Pastor, I can remember all of the odds that were against me. I was a young, black, female pastor in the south which wasn't any help at all! I can remember during this period of my life that there were key people in ministry who ended up leaving for various reasons known and unknown. There were a couple of times when I was at bible study that only one person showed up. How discouraging that was to my heart and spirit. I wanted to give up! I remember going to the pulpit to preach on Sundays and doing all it took to hold back the tears from the loneliness I felt. The enemy was making it as if I was a failure and nothing I was doing was working. The fasting, praying, and the seeking all seemed in vain. I remember going into worship with my tears of discouragement before I had to bring forth the word of God. However, God encouraged me each time and showed up in the midst of my discouragement.

During this period of time, I was supposed to get married, but God caused those plans to come to a halt. It was weeks before my wedding and God called it off. I also remember God allowing my best friend and me to separate after over 10 years of friendship. I felt like I wasn't connected to anyone and that I was all alone. I was basically by myself in the world; just like Elijah.

I knew my family loved me but I felt like I was at a place where no one else was. I had another friend but I felt like she couldn't even walk this stage of my life out with me. It was as if I was all alone and no one around me was experiencing what I was going through.

Had God forsaken me? Why did I have to walk such a lonely walk? How long would I have to preach and see no fruit? I remember being in my room crying out to the Lord. I began to remind him of the words he had spoken to me personally and through prophecy. I reminded him of how he had called me to the nations and his promise to me of international ministry. However, it seemed as if it was all to no avail. I cried myself to sleep many nights after lying prostrate before the Lord. I was determined not to give up but that didn't take away the pain of loneliness that seemed to reek relentlessly in my soul.

God would always send his confirming peace through a still small voice as he did with Elijah. However, there were times that I wanted him to speak to me in the great strong wind, the earthquake, Or the fire! I wanted his supernatural move to assure me that he was there. But as Elijah, he spoke to me in that still small voice and I had to get up and keep going.

I know that there are those out there reading this book that have felt some of these emotions. Perhaps even now you are experiencing some of the same feelings. We have to begin to understand and remember that God is the source of our life and without him at the center of our heart we will always remain empty. With God we are never alone. God has purposely created a space within man that only he can fill. We often hear this but if you think about it, all of us can still remember a time in our life where we have felt lonely. How many times have we wallowed in our loneliness saying, "No one understands me, no one cares about me, my husband or wife doesn't care about me, or I am all alone in this?"

As I have stated earlier, the Webster dictionary defines loneliness as lacking companionship and to be separated from or unfrequented by others. Loneliness is also having a feeling of depression or sadness resulting from the consciousness of being alone. This may very well be a good secular definition but there is more than meets the eye when it comes to understanding loneliness.

I want to say something key and profound in this next sentence that must be grabbed in your spirit if you are going to move from a place of loneliness to purpose. **Loneliness is not really loneliness, but destiny crying out in our souls to be fulfilled.** Wow! If we can ever grasp this statement and never let it go, we would always fight the spirit of loneliness that Satan tries to send our way. So read this statement 3 times out loud to yourself so that it is impended in your spirit. Say it: *"Loneliness is not really loneliness but destiny crying out in our souls to be fulfilled."*

We have to recognize that our natural mind only comprehends an unfulfilled God-given destiny as loneliness. Let us recognize that we are not really lonely which is lacking companionship, but we are longing. I would say longing is a prolonged, unfulfilled God given desire or need. When the longing in us isn't recognized and fulfilled, our mind and physical being recognizes it as loneliness. In order to deal with the lonely heart, we have to have a craving desire and aspiration for fulfilling our God-given purpose. When we have this craving desire and aspiration for fulfilling our God-given purpose, he will surround us with people and places that line up with where he desires to take us. He will remove those who hinder us and/or contribute towards the spirit of loneliness in our lives.

Whether we realize it or not, even being connected with the wrong person contributes to the spirit of loneliness that tries to creep up in our lives. Why is this true? Understand that these people aren't a part of your purpose and therefore are utilized by Satan to stop your destiny. Therefore, there remains a longing in your heart for the right relationship, a relationship that can only be formed when you are on the right track towards your purpose. Your spirit will long for fulfillment but just like the leech who is a parasitic bloodsucker that attaches itself to feed on the blood of birds, animals and humans, so is the relationship in your life that has nothing to do with pushing you towards your purpose. These relationships end up leaving you drained, empty, and void of purpose. It's time to get rid of the leeches in your life!

> *Loneliness is not really loneliness but destiny crying out in our souls to be fulfilled.*

Chapter 2

Everyone Has Needs

I can remember a season in my life where I was going through a very low stage because I had lost someone very dear to me. Although I thought I was okay, I began to see I wasn't okay by the decisions I was making. On the outside, I looked perfect to others. But on the inside, I was crumbling and there was a hole in my heart that I did not realize. I was making reckless decisions regardless of what I knew to be right and continued to justify what I did in order to make myself feel better for that period of time. At that time in my life, I was falling through what seemed to be an endless tunnel of destruction from which I could not escape. I remember feeling that I was a failure, worthless, and would never make anything out of my life. I remember the nights of constantly crying on my bed saying there has to be more to life. This was a time when depression and suicidal thoughts were a constant part of my life. I didn't realize that loneliness was the root cause of all of my experiences during this time.

I can even remember when I was younger; after experiencing sexual abuse as a child, I began to be very promiscuous and look for love in many places. To no avail, I would use sex as a tool for love that would heal the void and loneliness in my heart. I can remember satisfying my loneliness with a sexual remedy that was not working. The loneliness in my heart was only growing deeper.

No one wants to live a life of loneliness and everyone wants to be happy. The truth of the matter is that if we don't learn how to counteract loneliness, it will always be a constant nagging within our souls that longs to be fulfilled. Everyone needs to be able to believe that they can have a life free from loneliness. However, we often do not know how to obtain a life of hope and fulfillment.

I've come to realize that everyone has needs in life and we desire for those needs to be fulfilled. If these needs aren't fulfilled they will lead to loneliness. We can begin to understand something about these needs through Maslow's hierarchy of needs. You can find out more about these needs on line at Wikipedia. (en.wikipedia.org/wiki/Maslow's_hierarchy_of_needs)

During my sociological studies in college, I learned about Maslow's hierarchy of needs. Maslow discusses the five basic needs of man which start from the very basic need all the way to the highest need to be achieved. The five basic needs are physiological, safety, love/belonging, esteem and self-actualization.

The first stage is the physiological stage. This stage is where all humans basic needs begin. Maslow states that at this stage there are basic needs that must be met in order to live. These needs are breathing, food, water, sleep, homeostasis, excretion, and sex.

The second stage is safety. This stage is exemplified by the persons' need for security of the body, employment, resources, morality, family, health, and property.

The third stage is love/belonging. In this stage, you need to be loved and feel that you belong. In this stage there is the need for friendship, family, and sexual intimacy.

The fourth stage is esteem. In this stage, one attains self-esteem, confidence, achievement, respect for others, and respect by others.

The fifth stage is self-actualization. In this stage, Maslow's discusses that the person attains morality, creativity, spontaneity, problem solving abilities, lack of prejudice, acceptance of facts and need for privacy. In this stage the person focuses on self but for the greater good. This person is ethically strong, accepts short comings along with the good things about man. This person can be alone without human contact and do no harm to themselves. They often like solitude which helps them to regroup and become a better person. In this stage, the person realizes their full potential and it is reached. They become everything that one is capable of becoming. Maslow says that all previous needs must be met in order to reach this goal. A lot of people define this stage as achieving your purpose or destiny.

Maslow states that if stages 2-4 contain "deficiency needs" which are needs that have not been met within these stages, the body gives no physical indication but the individual feels anxious and tense. Although I don't agree 100% with a few of the concepts within some of the stages he mentions, Maslow has made a great theory and I believe it is one to be considered when dealing with loneliness. In my opinion, Maslow has hit the "nail on the head" when dealing with issues surrounding loneliness.

Loneliness is a big hindrance when it comes to achieving self-actualization in one's life. We know that self-actualization for one person may be totally different for another. However, it is true that loneliness cannot be a constant part of the picture when one is trying to get to the stage of self-actualization. We have to recognize that loneliness becomes a debilitating force that stunts our movement toward self-actualization. We all desire and want more out of life, but we often abort the destiny and promise due to us and never reach self-actualization.

I have created a little self-examination quiz in order for you to figure out where you are in your goal towards self-actualization, purpose, and destiny. First, take sections A and B of the quiz and examine where you are. Take your time on these quizzes; preferably spend at least one week on each need. So the first week you would work on the physiological need, the second week on the safety need and so on. You do not have to do them all at once. Some will go by quicker than others, but the goal of this quiz is for you to evaluate your life and make some changes that would push you toward your self-actualization, destiny, purpose or what many would call reaching your God-given ability. At the end of the book, you will go back and complete section C in order to re-order your steps towards self-actualization, destiny and purpose. Again take your time and do not rush through the quiz. Your goal is to make lasting changes in your life.

Chapter 3

Self-Assessment Quiz

*F*or each of the needs, go through and check yes if you have those needs completely fulfilled in your life. If any of the answers are no or somewhat, then explain why and what you can do to get those needs met, if possible. If it is not possible, what would be a satisfying alternative to this longing and desire? For example, a person may be a strong runner and feels a big part of achieving their self-actualization, destiny, and purpose is to be able to run a marathon. This may be very challenging because his or her physiological need of breathing isn't fully met. Due to his/her having asthma, it hinders them from being able to reach their purpose and they become frustrated, unfulfilled, and at times lonely.

These activities will help you look at what is hindering your process toward self-actualization, destiny and purpose. Only start out completing sections A & B and then at the end of the chapter come back and complete section C. Also, whatever you do, don't rush through the process. Carefully think about each need. Don't worry if you are having some problems answering every section. As you continue to seek God, his Holy Spirit will guide you eventually with the answers you need. Maybe upon completion of the book, God would have dropped some things in your spirit that you are able to come back to in this section and fill in your answers. In section C, if you were not able to fully give solutions for all of your answers then don't worry. Life is a journey and as you become more aware of whom you are and what you were created to become, through prayer, you will begin to receive the answers God has for you.

PHYSIOLOGICAL NEED

Physiological Need	Section (A.) Is This Need Met?	Section (B.) If No/ Somewhat then Why Not?	Section (C.) If No/Somewhat then What Can You Do...Is There A Safe and Healthy Alternative?
Do you have enough food daily?	☐ Yes ☐ No ☐ Somewhat		
Do you have enough clean water to drink and bathe in daily?	☐ Yes ☐ No ☐ Somewhat		
Do you get enough sleep to function properly on a day to day basis?	☐ Yes ☐ No ☐ Somewhat		
Homeostasis?	☐ Yes ☐ No ☐ Somewhat		
Excretion?	☐ Yes ☐ No ☐ Somewhat		
Healthy Sex Life?	☐ Yes ☐ No ☐ Somewhat		

SAFETY NEED

Safety Need	Is This Need Met?	If No/ Somewhat then Why Not?	If No/ Somewhat then What Can You Do…Is There A Safe and Healthy Alternative?
Your body is in a secure place, you are not in any place of physical threat or harm.	☐ Yes ☐ No ☐ Somewhat		
You are employed or are receiving a secure income.	☐ Yes ☐ No ☐ Somewhat		
You have resources to help you thrive in society.	☐ Yes ☐ No ☐ Somewhat		
You conform to the rules of right conduct in society; you display moral or virtuous conduct.	☐ Yes ☐ No ☐ Somewhat		

You have some type of family structure.	☐Yes ☐No ☐Somewhat		
You are in great health.	☐Yes ☐No ☐Somewhat		
You live in and/or have property that you consider valuable.	☐Yes ☐No ☐Somewhat		

LOVE AND BELONGING NEEDS

Love and Belonging Need	Is This Need Met?	If No/ Somewhat then Why Not?	If No/Somewhat then What Can You Do…Is There A Safe and Healthy Alternative?
Do you have at least one good friend or companion?	☐ Yes ☐ No ☐ Somewhat		
Do you have people that you consider to be your family? Family doesn't have to be biological.	☐ Yes ☐ No ☐ Somewhat		
Are you experiencing healthy sexual intimacy?	☐ Yes ☐ No ☐ Somewhat		
Do you feel like you belong to a supporting community?	☐ Yes ☐ No ☐ Somewhat		
Do you feel that you are love and accepted by others?	☐ Yes ☐ No ☐ Somewhat		

ESTEEM NEEDS

Esteem Needs	Is This Need Met?	If No/ Somewhat then Why Not?	If No/ Somewhat then What Can You Do…Is There A Safe and Healthy Alternative?
Do you have a realistic respect for or favorable impression of yourself? Do you feel good about yourself?	☐ Yes ☐ No ☐ Somewhat		
Do you believe in your power and ability to get things accomplished?	☐ Yes ☐ No ☐ Somewhat		
Do you believe that you have made several notable achievements in your life?	☐ Yes ☐ No ☐ Somewhat		
Do you have a hobby?	☐ Yes ☐ No ☐ Somewhat		
Do others recognize you as a major asset in their life?	☐ Yes ☐ No ☐ Somewhat		

SELF-ACTUALIZATION, PUPROSE AND DESTINY NEEDS

Self-Actualization, Purpose and Destiny Needs	Is This Need Met?	If No/ Somewhat then Why Not?	If No/ Somewhat then What Can You Do...Is There A Safe and Healthy Alternative?
Do you feel that your life has purpose?	☐ Yes ☐ No ☐ Somewhat		
Do you feel you know the purpose for which you were born?	☐ Yes ☐ No ☐ Somewhat		
Do you feel you are living out your life's purpose?	☐ Yes ☐ No ☐ Somewhat		
Do you have a sense of morality in your life?	☐ Yes ☐ No ☐ Somewhat		
Do you have your own unique form of creativity?	☐ Yes ☐ No ☐ Somewhat		
Are you good at solving your life's problems?	☐ Yes ☐ No ☐ Somewhat		

Are you free from prejudice of all races, sex, etc.	☐ Yes ☐ No ☐ Somewhat		
Are you readily able to accept the truth about yourself and use that to become a more productive person in society?	☐ Yes ☐ No ☐ Somewhat		
Are you able to take advantage of being alone at times?	☐ Yes ☐ No ☐ Somewhat		
Can you go out to eat by yourself and not feel strange?	☐ Yes ☐ No ☐ Somewhat		

Now that you have completed each of your own needs assessments in section A and B, we will move on to the next chapter. Hopefully you have not rushed through this exercise but have carefully thought out each of your needs. Remember at the end of the book you can work on section C of the needs assessment. This exercise will help you examine where you are and how you can move forward. Throughout the next chapters I will be making reference back to these needs and how we cannot allow these areas that are lacking to hinder us and lead us into a state of depression and loneliness.

Chapter 4

"Soul Food For Singles"

"Today was a challenging day and it is 8:34 p.m. on a Sunday evening. This morning service was powerful; God used me mightily to minister to the body of Christ. I could feel the anointing of God as I ministered to the church today. The sermon was entitled "I am well able to overcome." It was such a powerful message and the people were blessed. However, as I left the church I began to feel empty and I longed to have that physical soothing touch for my drained heart. What do I do? Where do I go? I am a single pastor and I don't have a husband to go home to. There is no one else here with me. I know God is here, but I have no physical touch."

This was a one year in my life, on a Sunday in January, when I decided to write in my journal. It was days like these where writing helped me to release my thoughts and feelings to God. This was a day that was really challenging for me but God helped me through as he always does. So what did I do you ask? I decided that instead of just sitting alone in a room feeling sorry for myself and focusing on being alone, I decided to turn my anguish and solace toward prayer. I decided to transfer my empty emotions into useful confessions in the spirit realm. I decided that instead of wasting time falling into sadness, I would channel those feelings into intercession for my destiny.

After deciding to push through in prayer my somber left and my comfort came!

Oftentimes, those who are single in ministry experience events such as this. However, whether single or married, we battle between the choices of depression, opportunities to settle for fleshly desires, or allowing self-pity to take over. We also have the choice to dismiss these emotions all together by channeling them into a greater purpose. This greater purpose can be prayer!

When these times of loneliness tends to try and overshadow us, we have to remember that we are really longing for God and longing for purpose in us to be filled. Yes, it may truly be a time where you just want to be around a physical body and may need to find family or friends to hang out with. But trust me there will be times when you will want a partner there and family or friends just won't cut it. So you have to focus your emotions on praying for purpose in your life to be filled as well as allowing your emotions to be placed upon the Lord. You have to emotionally and physically lay your emotions on God and see them being placed on him.

I have realized that being single doesn't mean that I have to waste time on somber emotions. Instead, I need to take a stand once and for all and push through my emotions to what has been promised for me ahead. If I don't, I will forever stay in a merry go round of "woe is me" emotions. Remember: You are graced to walk out the position you are in! If you are single you have been given the gift to walk out a successful single life and if you are married you have been graced to walk out a successful married life. Your job is to see what God considers success for you and walk it out.

I understand that this won't always be easy because it is so much easier to sulk in self-pity. However, if we truly want our souls to be fulfilled we have to get beyond our emotions and make a choice to get beyond our emotions. We have to make a choice to go forward in purpose whether we have someone or not. It's time to use our tongues to speak life into the empty places of our lives. It's time to fill the spirit realm with words that project us toward our future and then ask for wisdom on how to complete the work. We can't afford to compromise on holiness with the "pleasures of sin for a season." I have come too far and I recognize that it is not beneficial for me to go back. I've been there done that and can wear many t-shirts for it!

SINGLE WITH UNRESTRAINED EMOTIONS

I want to tell you about a time in my life when I met a man I will call "Bill." He was everything I wanted in a mate or so I thought. Whenever I was down he could always make me smile. I could always pick him up and knew when he was thinking about me. When we were together during the "intimate times", it was as if the passion was out of this world. It was as if we could hear what one another was thinking without either of us saying it and he had the attributes I was looking for in a man. He was a great friend, held intelligent conversations, looked good, smelled good, and was in church. So, I guess you are saying, "Girl what was wrong with you, why didn't you end up being with him." Well, simply put, it wasn't God's will.

First of all, did you catch one of the things that I said, "the passion was out of this world?" Okay, if I am a single Christian female, why was there passion? To put it simply, why was there sex outside of marriage? The average person would answer and say nothing is wrong with that, but to the contrary. I believe there is. I remember a preacher telling me one time and these were their words, "Honey you are a woman these things happen." I couldn't believe they had told me this. Yes I was a woman and will experience feelings but according to scripture I had to learn to put those feelings under subjection by the power of the Holy Spirit. If you are unsaved and reading this, you may say God understands. Yes God understands our feeling and wants to be there with us in our emotions, but he doesn't compromise in his word like we do. We are frail human beings and cannot control our sexual desires on our own without the help of God.

The average television shows today and back in the 90's glorified being single and having sex as a good thing. "Shacking" and sex were the icing on the cake for most of these relationships. There is one very popular sitcom in particular that promotes and glamorizes sex. One of the actor's in particular is a very sexually confident single woman who is considered a tri-sexual. She will "try" anything once." It is important to note that the Washington post online referenced a 2008 study published in the *Journal of American Academy of Pediatrics.* They found that females 12-17 who watched these, and similarly "sexually charged" shows were about twice as likely to get pregnant as those who did not, and teenage male viewers were more likely to impregnate someone. These shows glorify sex and do very little on giving important information about pregnancy and sexually transmitted diseases. (Washington Post 2008)

I have personally encountered countless teens in my profession of teen pregnancy prevention that have contracted sexually transmitted diseases through "un-protected sex and one night stands." Some of these boys and girls were as young as 12 years of age.

As I discussed earlier, Maslow's hierarchy of needs stated that in order to reach self-actualization, one has to have the need of sex and sexual intimacy met. Here is where I disagree to an extent. Because I live according to the word of God, it clearly states that we are not to participate in sexual relations outside of marriage. Yes our bodies are biological and we all have sexual needs but we have to learn to take control of these sexual needs and urges. We have to learn how to bring these desires under the subjection of the Holy Spirit. This can be very challenging but if we are going to live a life holy and pleasing to God then this should be our aim. No matter how hard the challenge it can be done. This is not to say that my body no longer biologically craves sex, but I'm saying it takes power with God and self-control. I will discuss how later on. Paul gives us an example below:

Romans 7:19-25 says, *"For what I do is not the good I want to do; no, the evil I do not want to do—this I keep on doing. Now if I do what I do not want to do, it is no longer I who do it, but it is sin living in me that does it. So I find this law at work: When I want to do good, evil is right there with me. For in my inner being I delight in God's law, but I see another law at work in the members of my body, waging war against the law of my mind and making me a prisoner of the law of sin at work within my members. What a wretched man I am! Who will rescue me from this body of death? Thanks be to God—through Jesus Christ our Lord! So then, I myself in my mind am a slave to God's law, but in the sinful nature a slave to the law of sin."*

Paul describes the battle of the flesh so eloquently here. If we don't get our bodies under subjection to the Holy Spirit and allow him to help us in controlling our sexual desires as singles, we will constantly be a slave to our fleshly bodies. We will allow our bodies to control us verses the Holy

Spirit controlling us. We have to learn how to live more in the spirit realm verses only in the soulish realm with our soulish desires. That soulish part of us lives out of the seat of our appetites, mind, will and our emotional self. Our soulish realm deals more with the emotional part of our human nature. When we have sex outside of marriage we make soul-ties that keep us bound to the individual and therefore we take on their spirit and personality. There is a connection that goes on in each soul that becomes hard to break. This is why even though the relationship may not be ordained of God, one can still feel a strong tie and connection that they think is right.

I know we hear a lot about finding our "soul-mate" but we need to not only find our soul-mate but our divinely ordained connection. If we are not careful we will choose the mate that feels right to our flesh or soul but not necessarily connect with the person that is a part of our God given destiny!

Does the person line up with where you know your purpose lies or are they just fulfilling a need for where you are now? This is why you need to make sure that you are constantly moving toward a place spiritually for where God wants you to be. You will attract where you are and where you are vulnerable. If you are goal oriented and focused on your destiny, the opportunity for those who line up with your destiny will be there in God's timing. True enough there will be those that come your way that are not a part of your destiny but when you are focused you won't settle. Satan will never stop sending someone to try and sidetrack your destiny. It is when we get weak and impatient that we often settle or fall with those who are not necessarily heading in the same direction of potential that we are. Always remember, a person who may qualify for where you are now may not be qualified to walk with you once you decide to walk into your purpose. This is very tricky and it takes a great deal of prayer and discernment because if we are not careful we will be deceived and mistaken. We will choose a person because it "feels" right but we have to recognize that we can't base the relationship on feelings alone. Basing a relationship on feelings alone will almost always get us into trouble. Therefore, always choose to walk in your purpose with God and he won't let you down. You have to be so comfortable with just you and God that if your mate comes that is fine and if he doesn't that's fine too.

In my relationship with "Bill", I was basing my relationship on my loneliness and wanting a man to hold, to smell, to have intelligent conversation with and to love him as much as I could. There is nothing wrong with wanting these attributes in a partner, however, I was doing it illegally and the relationship wasn't of God. We were good friends and I could talk to him about anything. He would tell me how much he loved me and how he wanted me to marry him when he, as he put it, "took care of some things that he needed to take care of in his life." I knew he wasn't the one God had called me to be with. You may ask how I knew he wasn't, but trust me; I knew he wasn't who God wanted for me, outside of sex, outside of marriage there were some other things he had going on. There were many times I would try to justify my sin and why I was with him. I would try to talk myself into believing he might be "the one." The truth is… I loved the sex and I just felt like I was going through so much in my life during that time that I just needed to get my sexual needs met. I thought that at least it helped me feel better for the moment. I felt I needed the intimacy. I would be sorry, feel miserable for sinning and regretted it afterwards but at least I had a temporary fix for my emotions. But eventually that got old and I could no longer take the hole that it left in my heart each time I was finished. If you have a true desire to please the Lord but struggle in these types of relationships, then you will be constantly drained emotionally. These relationships always suck the life out of your spirit and keep you from fulfilling purpose.

Please stop and recognize this point, if you have to justify to yourself why that person is in your life, this is a clear sign that he or she may not be the one for you. When that person is the one that is a part of your destiny, no justification will be needed because you will have a witness in yourself from the Lord that he or she is the one. There will be a knowing that he or she is the one. You won't have to constantly wonder. Even though I am single, I believe this whole heartedly because this is what God ministered to me in my prayer time with him. However, remember that healthy questioning is always acceptable in a relationship because everyone should be well informed on what they may walk into when it comes to relationships. When you are close to God, even if the individual you are dating tries to mislead you, the Holy Spirit will put a witness in your spirit and let you know. You will have that discernment and knowing that something isn't right. This is why I was almost married twice and it was cancelled. I was moving in my selfish desires and not God's desire for my life. However, because of my prayers and relationship with him, he wouldn't let me go through with either of them. It wasn't fear of getting into a relationship but it was the fear of God in me keeping me from it.

Another big sign that "Bill" wasn't for me was that he was not able to communicate to me effectively concerning why he felt I was the one for him. When I asked him where he sees our relationship going in God and how our future with God would be in the relationship, he couldn't answer. He was saved, so he should have been able to give some type of answer. Your potential mate may not have a complete idea of where both of you are to go in the future concerning your destinies together, but there should be a mutual confirming agreement. If the person has no clue whatsoever, give them time to go and seek the Lord and come back with an answer. If after a month they aren't able to answer you and continue to give excuses, then you may want to reconsider if this is the one for you. If you are as important as they say you are, they will be eager to seek God and find out. Also, if the person comes back with an answer that's completely opposite of where you know God has called you then keep moving. Remember, allow God to give you the strength to wait or you can settle the choice is yours.

For example, if God has said that you are to be one who is to devote your life toward missions and the one you are with says they are horrified about going overseas and can't stand missions; you may want to reconsider if this person is the one that will join you in your destiny.

Here are a few other clues that may indicate that the person you are with may not be the one you are suppose to share your God given destiny with. First of all, if it goes against biblical principles this is a big red flag. I'm sure that some may not agree with this statement but this is my observation and opinion. Is sex the basis of the relationship? Is adultery being committed? Is the relationship based on selfish reasons? If any of these are true then you should definitely re-evaluate the relationship. These are just a few main reasons that need to be looked at in a potential relationship.

SINGLES CHOOSE CAREFULLY

When I graduated from college and began to work in Teen Pregnancy Prevention, I worked with a group of girls who I had to mentor and teach concerning the risks of sex. Well, I wasn't the normal teen pregnancy prevention teacher because although I discussed the risks that go along with sex, information on contraception and decision making skills, they also knew I was a Christian. So, when they would want me to turn the radio on, there were stipulations on what they could listen to. Anyway, one day they wanted me to listen to this song on the radio called "No Scrub." Well at the time I had not heard the lyrics at all but the youth were trying to convince me that it was a good song to listen to. So, when I did, to my surprise it was good. If you haven't heard it before I encourage you to look up the lyrics or listen to it. It's a really good portrayal of who you don't want to be with.

Let me stop here and say that I'm not bashing men because there are definitely female scrubs out there! As one of my mentor's call them, "Chicken Heads." So whether it is a "scrub" or a "chicken head", there are many of these in the body of Christ! You can't afford to have anyone in your life that is just there for the ride and to get all they can out of you. If they don't have anything to add to the relationship nor has anything but empty promises you better keep it moving. Our goal as singles in ministry is to not become nor date one of these because it will hinder our purpose. The spirit of a "scrub" or a "chicken head" will try to derail you from your destiny and encountering your true mate!

I can remember two times in my life where I was engaged and God called it off. I can remember one of my friends asking another friend what was wrong with me now. Others were saying, "She called the wedding off again." What was wrong with me was that I was not willing to settle for less. God knows who he has for us and we have to refuse to settle!

I can truly say that during a season in my life I was really in love with one individual in particular and really thought he was the one but God cut it off. We weren't engaged but things happened and it ended. In another relationship, I just wasn't ready; there were issues in my life that needed to be dealt with. In the last relationship that I cancelled a week before the wedding, God had called this one off as well.

Here are several things that I did in the relationships that I knew were not going to work. First, I was dating a Christian but we were still unequally yoked. The individual that I was with was very young in the spirit and I was a minister. They were intrigued with my ministry but not wholeheartedly in me. I naively thought that because he was young in the spirit that I could train him to be my mate. Wrong thinking! He did and said anything he thought I wanted to hear but didn't have any ambitions of his own. It was as if I had to make all of the decisions and do all of the planning. Men are to be the head in marriage and not the tail. So I got tired of that! Plus there were some things going on behind the scenes that I found out later that I had been suspicious about.

During my first engagement, I brought residue from a past relationship into this one. Ladies and gentleman, we have to let go of the old before we can move into the new. I was trying to run out of one toxic relationship into another. I was in this relationship because I liked him but wasn't truly in love with him. At first I felt like he was a good person and I thought about how I was getting older. I thought it could work because he was a preacher and I was a preacher. I also thought about how we both loved God and so I just assumed it had to work. However, these things are definitely not enough. All major issues in each individual have to be dealt with before it can work. Now I'm not saying that each person will be completely perfect but there are some things that each person knows about themselves that need to be worked on. Then they will not bring that baggage into another relationship.

Also in this relationship, I noticed that the he had a temper. It was something about him that kept reminding me of someone I knew that had a temper. I couldn't put my finger on it but I knew I was discerning something. Well…. come to find out, he ended up sharing with me that his mother was in an abusive relationship by his father for many years. However, what really sent me running and not looking back was a statement that he made to me. He told me and I quote… "If you ever cheated on me and I caught you in the act, I would shoot you and him then both of you would go straight to hell because both of you would die and not have time to repent." Okay…. when he said that, I was thinking to myself …oh no it is over!!! What kind of minister would say such a thing?!?!

So, I want to end this section by telling you not to ignore the warning signs that go on inside of you concerning individuals you are considering spending a lifetime with. If you feel or see any red flags in the relationship then get out! There are many fish in the sea so choose carefully. God has given us wisdom and we must use that wisdom when it comes to selecting or accepting a mate. In the next chapter we will talk about different aspects of relationships through the eyes of men and women.

Chapter 5

Men Verses Women
In Relationships

Why does it seem that woman carry more emotional baggage than men in relationships? I have talked with countless women who have been in and out of relationships, but yet they still seem to hold some emotional baggage from the relationship. This statement tends to hold truth especially when sex is involved. Like it or not, there are many Christians who are sexually active or participating in some type of sexual activity prior to marriage. I believe this prior sexual activity leads up to periods of loneliness after the sexual encounters are over.

In this chapter, I want to briefly discuss men verses women in relationships because I believe that it will be helpful in understanding the sexes. I interviewed several men and women, all from various cultures and backgrounds, in order to obtain their views on dealing with relationships and sex. Prayerfully, this section will help you understand yourself and how to identify a suitable mate.

As men and women of God, we need to seek to please God ultimately if we ever expect to have the mate God desires for us. Are there relationships that are not Godly but successful? Of course there are. But I am specifically addressing Christians because more and more Christians are remaining single for longer periods of time.

I interviewed several people from various cultures and backgrounds in order to obtain answers to four main questions. Out of the questions asked, I chose the most popular responses.

1. Do you think that women tend to be more emotional than men when it comes to sex? Why or why not? 2. Do you think single Christian men feel the same amount of remorse and guilt after they have had sex as a female would? Why or why not? 3. If a man has had sex outside of marriage with someone, how likely do you think it will be for him to marry that person? Give your answer in percentages from one to 100%. Why did you answer this way? 4. As a single man or woman, what are your five "must haves" in a potential mate? In other words, they must possess these five qualities/characteristics before you will marry them.

After conducting the survey, I obtained various responses that were helpful. The answers were candidly provided by both single and married people. In order to provide an unbiased view, the people interviewed ranged from those who considered themselves to be strong Christians to those that love God but need a lot of work.

Question 1: Do you think that women tend to be more emotional than men when it comes to sex? Why or Why not?

African American male in his mid-twenties: "*I think that most women are more emotional with sex than men because men can have sex without the emotional attachment. It's almost like a game we men play sometimes for bragging rights. Some others are like a junky's simply looking for another fix. While women are* *catching feeling with make-believe character whose out to accomplish one goal, the goods."*

Asian Female in her mid to late twenties: *"I honestly don't know. I've never had sex before. I have no idea what it is like. Growing up in China, we don't teach anything about that either...women in general are much more emotional than men. So why would sex be an exception anyway."*

African American Female in her thirties: *"Yes, I feel women are more emotional than men, it's part of our makeup. When a woman finds a man she is interested in, she catches feelings for him and becomes attached. A man is still in his 'We're just Friends Mode.' Men can detach faster because they're not as emotional. Look at this way; in the midst of intimacy when a man reaches that peak, he does what-pull out! It's part of his make up!"*

Caucasian Male in his forties: *"In general, I think women are more emotional about sex because they put more emotions into sex. They personalize it more as a consummation of a relationship. I think that younger generation females have been able to generalize sex more. Women have become more aggressive it seems to me."*

Caucasian Female teenager: *"Yes, I believe that as a single teenager we sometimes get attached feelings to the boy when we never meant to get those feelings in the first place. I feel like some boys don't care as long as there 'getting what they want" And girls get the worthless and not good enough feelings unlike the boy. And for me personally, I know it's harder to get over things like that."*

African American Male in his late thirties: *"Yes I do feel that women become more emotionally attached after sexual activity. My reason for my opinion is because by nature women are carriers and I personally feel that when a woman goes to the degree of* *giving her body, she is giving of her emotions also, which causes her to carry that moment of intercourse as a hope for something more."*

Caucasian Female in her Mid-twenties: *"Yes. I think this is due to it being ingrained into women that we must wait until we find "the one," and have it emphasized to us in our youth that sex is meant to be a romantic endeavor. Women are more emotional creatures to begin with and are taught to focus on the emotional connections that come with sex. To the contrary, men are taught less about the personal connections that are created with sex and more with the focus of "be careful, don't get her pregnant."*

Question 2: Do you think single Christian men feel the same amount of remorse and guilt after they have had sex as a single Christian female? Why or Why not?

African American male in his mid-twenties: *"I think that the remorse depends on your walk with Christ. Just as the disciples walked with Jesus and grew stronger so should the man or woman. If you are distant from Jesus, then it is easier to sin no matter who you are."*

Asian Female in her mid to late twenties: *"Gosh, I really don't have the answer as I've never experienced it and never even talked to a guy about sex..."*

African American Female in her thirties: *"No, I don't feel that men feel more guilty or remorseful after they have sex before marriage but, if he is a Christian, he should feel guilty and remorseful because, it's not right. You have to stand your ground when it comes to (Slip ups) because it's easy to get in that we already sinned so we may as well keep on doing it mode. When it comes to the opposite sex, SEX PLAYS A HUGE PART! Men are more sensitive but women are more emotional."*

Caucasian Male in his forties: *"I think that sex before marriage these days produces little guilt to either gender. The guilt may be associated with getting pregnant or caught but sex before marriage has become very common even among Christians. Look at the royalty in England that just got married. They have been living together for ten years so I assume they have had sex which I think has been determined."*

Caucasian Female teenager: *"Yes, I believe if a boy or girl has a strong walk with the Lord, then they will have the same guilt! I believe if we are Christians and God says not to do it and we disobey then we're all going to feel guilty."*

African American Male in his late thirties: *"No I do not believe that the single Christian males are as remorseful as the single Christian females are after sex. My reason is because most of the time for the male, the remorse doesn't come unless the female ends up pregnant and in some cases it's the same for both."*

White Female in her mid-twenties: *"No. Men and women have different social pressures when it comes to sex. As I said above, women are taught to focus on the romance involved. Women are also made out to be sluts or other negative things as soon as they begin having sex. It is impressed upon women to guard their sexuality and that they are morally unsound if they don't. Men on the other hand are encouraged to be womanizers. The terms associated with men who have multiple sexual partners are usually positive or that of triumph. When discussing sex, men are congratulated and women are made to feel guilty. It's one of the greatest social double standards our society faces."*

Question 3: If a man has had sex outside of marriage with someone, how likely do you think he will marry that person? Give answers in percentages from 1 to 100%. Why did you answer this way?

African American male in his mid-twenties: *"I think that the man is about 15% likely to marry the other person because the outside fling is just a quick fix. It is meaningless- just a break from the norm. It may be a game to see if he still got it. If the wife finds out and leave then the percentage increase to about 85% because guys hate to be alone. So we settle for the next best thing."*

Asian Female in her mid to late twenties: *"Outside of the marriage... If for my guess, and based on my reading, not likely - 10%? Or even less."*

African American Female in her thirties: *"I feel it is 50/50% because, I've seen it go both ways. I feel like the condition of the marriage, maturity and why he cheated plays a huge part. I guess it depends on where his head is at-mentally! Situations like this re-mind me of the 80/20 rule that Jakes talk's about-It's not always Greener on the other Side!"*

Caucasian Male in his forties: *"I believe 10%. People have sex outside of marriage because they are not getting the sexual attention they want. The person usually, in my experience, does not intend to dissolve the marriage they are currently in. They're just receiving the attention they desire from their spouse from an alternative person."*

Caucasian Female teenager: *"50% because you're taking a lot of risks by having sex. If you end up marrying that person, it might be for the wrong reason (unplanned pregnancy). I also believe there is a small chance of marrying that person because you have nothing to look forward to."*

African American Male in his late thirties: *I think 50% of the men who are sexually active outside of marriage will get married. I say 50 % because most end up getting married because of the female getting pregnant.*

Caucasian Female in her mid-twenties: "*20% most men I know have had an average of 4 or 5 sexual partners in their lives.*"

Question 4: As a single man/woman what are your five "must haves" in a potential mate? If you are married, what are five attributes do you desire/like to have in your mate?

African American male in his mid-twenties: "*She must be saved, must have faith, must be a tither and a giver, must have style and class and she must be educated.*"

Asian Female in her mid to late twenties: "*Finally there is something I can answer!!! 1) Love God -obviously meaning having a relationship with the Lord. 2) Adventurous enough that he would go and do whatever God calls him to go/do. 3) Hard working - this is so important. He must have good work ethics. This demonstrates integrity and trustworthiness. 4) Good looking in 'my' eyes and not necessarily everyone else. After all, I have to be living with him for the rest of my life. 5) Hmmm, I feel the four would be enough. I'll throw just one then - he cares for me personally.*"

African American Female in her thirties: "*1) He must be saved, loving, affectionate, sanctified, Holy Ghost filled and Understands Ministry and Kingdom Principals. 2) He must be a LEADER in Every Aspect but knows how to be a team Player (Supportive in all that I do). 3) He must be able to provide comfortably for his Family and be a successful working man. 4) Able to communicate to me with complete honesty regardless of what's going on. 5) He has to love God more than he loves me. I'm only willing to come second to GOD!*"

Caucasian Male in his forties: "*I need to be attracted to her, intelligent, funny, trustworthy, Christian.*"

Caucasian Female teenager: "*1) Respects me in all areas. 2) Has goals & motives. 3) Loves the Lord & most of all, his family. 4) Loves me for who I am. 5) I need to be attracted to him.*"

African American Male in his late thirties: "*1) She must be saved. 2) A lady, know how to carry herself in private as well as in public. 3) Appealing to my attractions; not just physical either. 4) Supportive of my aspirations. 5) Know how to take care of a home.*"

Caucasian Female in her mid-twenties: "*1) Compatible sense of humor. 2) Supports my major life decisions. 3) Encourages me promotes the best in me. 4) Makes me aware of my faults with a focus on improvement, not reprimand. 5) Treats me as a partner and friend.*"

After reading the survey responses, I ask that you take time to reflect on them and to identify where you are personally. Once you have done this, you need to be truthful with yourself and with God if you plan to move on to a healthy relationship. In essence, a relationship that is healthy for you in the eyes of God.

Reflection Questions

1. What are some major differences that you see when it comes to men and women in relationships?

2. Take a few minutes and ask God to reveal to you any weaknesses in your life regarding your desires for the opposite sex. After he reveals them, ask him to give you a strategy to become stronger in that area.

Chapter 6

Lust Verses Love

It truly feels good to have those in your life who love you with no agenda or ulterior motive. With all of the lust and deception in the world, to experience this kind of love is a refreshing thing. It is truly amazing when you have people in your life that just love you for you. This kind of love comes rarely. When you find people who are showing that genuine kind of love, you want to hold onto them for dear life because they are showing the love of God through their very being. We truly need to experience more of this true love in the earth.

Satan relentlessly attacks genuine love. He continues to do whatever he can to distort God-given love. He often seems to operate at his strongest through the spirit of loneliness. We can see his attacks through various acts such as adultery, fornication, molestation, pornography, and abuse. When you are truly in love with someone, you don't want to do anything that would jeopardize or damage their life. You will always seek to cover and protect them at any cost and sometimes that cost means denying your own selfish desires which may lead to something that is deceitful. You cannot afford to operate off of how you feel but you must operate off of what you know to be right.

In this chapter, my goal is to explain what true love is and what it is not. You will understand the difference between love and lust; see how Satan tries to contaminate love in the earth and learn how to recognize his deception.

Senses of the Flesh

When we were in elementary school, we were taught about the five physical senses which are hearing, seeing, touching, smelling and tasting. We were taught that these senses allow us to interact and perceive in our society. Our five senses have guided us throughout our lives. All of these senses are connected to our physical and spiritual body. I will share a few examples of this.

Picture the sound of rain watering the earth, the beautiful sight of the sun as it sets below the horizon in beautiful array; the warm embrace of a mother's love as she strokes her infant; the smell of freshly squeezed ice cold lemonade on hot summer day; and the taste of warm glazed maple syrup over golden pancakes. These are all ways many of us have incorporated our five senses.

Now let's picture ruptured ear drums from listening to music to loud; the sight of a husband who can't sleep with his wife because he is addicted to the pornography he watches on the computer; the excruciating pains of a child who has experienced third degree burns from being drenched in hot water by their mother; the smell of cologne on an adulterous partner as they sneak back home to shower after a night of infidelity; or the painful taste of sores in one's mouth after receiving massive doses of chemotherapy treatment.

These are many powerful ways to connect to the world through our senses, but too much indulgence or misuse of the five senses can be damaging to our physical, emotional, and spiritual health.

I used these examples in order to show you how what you do in the physical affects what happens to you emotionally and spiritually. I'm sure you felt emotions or had thoughts from what you were asked to picture. This was to trigger a response in your emotional realm in order to let you know that we have to guard your physical senses. If we do not guard our physical senses, then it will corrupt our spiritual and emotional senses as well. This in turn will affect other decisions we make in life especially when it comes to love and lust. I specifically want to focus on the distinction between lust and love.

When I used to teach teen pregnancy prevention, we had to do an activity where I asked the youth to name all the words they could for three different words. The first word was sex, the second was body parts and then the final was love. The youth had no problem giving me countless number of slang terms when it came to slang names for sex and the body parts but when it came to explaining love, they could not do it. Many say that teenagers are too young to know what love is and that may be true. However, I also believe that it is our responsibility as adults to explain to our youth what true love is and what it is not.

After completing this exercise, I would always ask the youth if they were to take the sex out of the relationship what fun would be left. Often times, the boys would say that they couldn't do it and that the relationship wouldn't be fun anymore. When I asked the girls, they would often give the same statement as the boys. However, the girls more oftentimes than boys would equate sex with love.

The problem stems from the fact that most adults don't always know what true love is. They spend most of their lives going through life experimenting on what they think love is. This is why we see so much confusion with the understanding of true love verses fleshly desires. If we are ever going to grab a hold of healthy love relationships, we first have to understand what true love is.

Sex and love are not the same. Sex is the gratification of the flesh that gives physical pleasure. The purpose of sex is for pure gratification and emotional connectedness. So you don't have to be in love to have sex but you can be in love and have sex.

Understand that sex can go more in line with lust although it isn't always lust. The Greek word for lust is porneu which means to act as the harlot, to indulge in unlawful lust/sex or to commit fornication (Strong's Concordance Online). When a person is in lust, they act as a harlot who is a person who sleeps around; they also often change from partner to partner seeking fleshly gratification. They have no physical control over their own body.

As Christians and non-Christians it is important to understand that we have to always stick with the truth. This truth is God and his word. If we choose to line up with the commandments of the word of God then we will not fall prey to deception.

The truth from the bible gives me a clear understanding of what true love is. For reference, I desire to use the scripture from 1 Corinthians 13:4-8 which says:

"Love is patient, love is kind. It does not envy, it does not boast, it is not proud. It does not dishonor others, it is not self-seeking, it is

not easily angered, it keeps no record of wrongs. Love does not delight in evil but rejoices with the truth. It always protects, always trusts, always hopes, always perseveres. Love never fails" (NIV).

I want to point out from this particular scripture several things that love does not do. This can be your indicator in a relationship when you are trying to decide which relationships are right for you. These five points will be indicators to show you if you are truly in love or in deception of the flesh.

- **Love does not dishonor others:**

    This comes in handy especially if you have been, or thinking about being in adulterous relationship. Anytime you are involved in an extra-marital affair, you are sowing seeds of discord and bringing dishonor upon yourself and the other party. It is a disgrace and a shame to the victims involved. You have to prefer the welfare of others instead of trying to receive your own private advantage. There is no true love in an adulterous relationship only deception!

    Adulterous relationships always seem to be intriguing, exciting, adventurous, and full of passion. You and your adulterous partner appear to be made for each other but this only leads to deceit. Nine times out of 10 if you had to live with this person, the relationship would not last. This is because you only see the adulterous partner a percentage of the time. Living with this person would be entirely different.

    However, there is a rush that the adulterous partners get from being in the relationship. The relationship holds an intriguing hidden secret. It is the nature of the soul and flesh that is thriving throughout this relationship. I believe Romans Chapter 8:5-8 explains this clearly. It says:

"Those who live according to the sinful nature have their minds set on what that nature desires; but those who live in accordance with the Spirit have their minds set on what the Spirit desires. The mind of sinful man is death, but the mind controlled by the Spirit is life and peace; the sinful mind is hostile to God. It does not submit to God's law, nor can it do so. Those controlled by the sinful nature cannot please God "(NIV).

Our sinful nature will always be in strong opposition with God, and Satan will do his best to make sure that we are constantly operating in this sinful nature. This is why it is important for us to have our minds renewed in the word of God and to also make sure that our relationship with God is strong. If we do not have a strong relationship with God then we are at risk for failure when it comes to relationships. He is the ultimate guide on relationships because he knows what is best for us. We should always include him in on our relationships so that we will know we have the person God desires for us.

If you are a single Christian having sex outside of marriage, you are dishonoring yourself, God and living a life of deception. Sex outside of marriage isn't love but lustful and self-seeking.

- **<u>Love is not self-seeking</u>:**

  Again, sex outside of marriage is self-seeking because you are taking care of your own needs verses God's needs and desires for your life. Self-seeking relationships can never know or give true love because it's always about what "I" can get out of it. It is just the gratification of the flesh to make one self feel better for the moment. It does not think about the consequences later, but enjoys the satisfaction of what "I" can get out of it right now.

As Christians, we should be like Moses in Hebrews 11:24-26. It says, *"By faith Moses, when he was come to years, refused to be called the son of Pharaoh's daughter; Choosing rather to suffer affliction with the people of God, than to enjoy the pleasures of sin for a season; Esteeming the reproach of Christ greater riches than the treasures in Egypt: for he had respect unto the recompense of the reward."*

As Christians, we have to decide whether we want to live in love or under deception. Do we want to enjoy the pleasures of sin for a season verses the riches in Christ.

We have to choose to live in the spirit of love and not the spirit of deception. The spirit of deception is a very powerful spirit because it appeals to the lust of the flesh and the five senses we talked about earlier. If the word of God isn't instilled in us and we don't have a firm relationship bonded with the creator; then the more susceptible we will be to deception.

What is deception? According to the online dictionary, the word deception means to deceive. To deceive means to mislead by false appearance or statement. It also means to be unfaithful to one spouse, to delude, to mislead or falsely persuade others. It also means to entrap, to ensnare, or betray. Deception is anything opposite of the truth.

If you can find any of these characteristics in your relationship then you are not operating in true love but deception. There is no way to sugarcoat it; the truth is just the truth. Until we are able to be true with ourselves and the relationships we are in, we will never enter into a relationship that God has for us. We will constantly find ourselves in relationships that leave us with a broken heart. These relationships will continue to be unfruitful, unproductive, and detrimental to our souls.

This is the time to stop selling ourselves cheap. It is time for us to mature in Christ and live according to his perfect will. We will only begin to do this when we stop deceiving ourselves and living a lie.

True love stands on what it knows to be right and not on what it feels. Remember your feelings will always get you into trouble. We have to make a conscious decision to live for truth. True love means that I let go of my own selfish desires in order to live for God's desires.

God desires for us to be healthy and whole in all of our relationships. He doesn't want any of our relationships to be fragmented.

As long as we live in this world, we will always be challenged in our relationships. There will be many times when our flesh will long and crave for needs that are opposite of God's will. There will also be times when Satan himself will release an ongoing attack on your physical body. He will make it seem as if you owe it to your flesh to fulfill its lustful desires. If we are not careful to recognize Satan's tactics, he will make us feel like we have insatiable desires that have to be quenched. We would then end up fulfilling these insatiable desires and become trapped in a never ending cycle of deceit.

No matter how you put it, sex outside of what God has intended will always lead to deceit. For example, when a person is committing fornication, he or she may know that the relationship is wrong but because of the strongholds formed in this relationship it is hard to get out. These strongholds will make you feel as if you and the other person are meant to be together. It will feel as if you both are flowing in this same vein. However, Satan has you bound and there has been a veil of deceit placed over your spirit. Until you come in contact with and recognize the truth, this veil will remain.

The veil of deceit will be removed when we let go of our own selfish desires.

- **<u>Love always protects</u>**

Love protects in a way which defends and guards from attack or loss. This attack and loss can be physical, emotional, or spiritual. It covers and shield's from danger.

Physical attack would be any attack on that person's body. Emotional attack would be anything that affects a person's state of consciousness in a negative way; it is the agitation of the feelings that could cause anger, regret, or hate. Spiritual attack would be anything that causes the person to act in direct opposite of what they morally know to be right.

When you say that you love someone, are you willing to guard them from the attacks of the enemy? What can the enemy use in order to get between the love you have for that person? Are you willing to fight in order to make sure you are not the vessel Satan uses to attack that person? Again this attack can be physical, emotional, or spiritual.

- **<u>Love never fails</u>**

    There is only one person in the world that can love us unconditionally and their love will never fail and that is God. His love never fails! When everyone else's love fails, his continues to remain past the end of time.

    We as people are frail human beings in our own selves but with Christ we are able to overcome.

    Even after all of our mistakes of the past, our times of unfaithfulness to him, our disobedience and continued indulgence in selfish ways, God's unmerited mercy and love never fails. We don't deserve his love but he gives it anyway. When we feel unlovable he still loves us. His love is unfathomable, indescribable, and immeasurable, his love never fails. When we give up on ourselves he never does.

Man will fail us with his love but God's love can't be compared with any other. No matter how much we try to love as God loves we will never be able to love like he loves completely because he is perfect love. As his spirit lives within us we can begin to share in this perfect love. However, the more we seek him the closer we can begin to experience and give this type of love.

In every trial, every test, every trouble, every victory, every failure, and every defeat, God continues to remind me of my need for his unmerited love. The more we fail him the more he yearns to pour out his love upon us and to reveal his perfect love. There is no love greater than his love. His love never fails!

I'm reminded of 2 Corinthians 4:7-12 which says,

"But we have this treasure in earthen vessels, that the excellency of the power may be of God, and not of us. We are troubled on every side, yet not distressed; we are perplexed, but not in despair; Persecuted, but not forsaken; cast down, but not destroyed; Always bearing about in the body the dying of the Lord Jesus, that the life also of Jesus might be made manifest in our body. For we which live are always delivered unto death for Jesus' sake, that the life also of Jesus might be made manifest in our mortal flesh. So then death worketh in us, but life in you."

No matter what we go through God's love is always there! The death of his son on the cross proves his unlimited love for us. We see this in St. John 3:16 *"For God so loved the world, that he gave his only begotten Son, that whosoever believeth in him should not perish, but have everlasting life."*

Jesus gave us his love by sending his son to die for our sins and our fallible ways because he is infallible. His love is infallible.

Reflection Questions

1. In what areas do you feel like you have fallen short when it comes to love and how do you desire to change that?

2. Have you ever substituted lust for love in your life, and if so, how do you plan to avoid the pitfalls of falling into lust again?

Chapter 7

Controlling The Desires Of The Body

I want to begin this chapter by opening up with some good advice that I believe Paul gives to the singles and married couples in ministry.

It comes from 1 Corinthians 7 which says,

"Now for the matters you wrote about: It is good for a man not to marry... But since there is so much immorality, each man should have his own wife, and each woman her own husband... I say this as a concession, not as a command... I wish that all men were as I am. But each man has his own gift from God; one has this gift, another has that... Now to the unmarried and the widows I say: It is good for them to stay unmarried, as I am... But if they cannot control themselves, they should marry, for it is better to marry than to burn with passion... Nevertheless, each one should retain the place in life that the Lord assigned to him and to which God has called him. This is the rule I lay down in all the churches... Circumcision is nothing and uncircumcision is nothing. Keeping God's commands is what counts... Each one should remain in the situation which he was in when God called him... Brothers, each man, as responsible to God, should remain in the situation God called him to. Now about virgins: I have no command from the Lord, but I give a judgment as one who by the Lord's mercy is trustworthy... Because of the present crisis, I think that it is good for you to remain as you are... Are you married? Do not seek a divorce. Are you unmarried? Do not look for a wife... But if you

do marry, you have not sinned; and if a virgin marries, she has not sinned. But those who marry will face many troubles in this life, and I want to spare you this... What I mean, brothers, is that the time is short. From now on those who have wives should live as if they had none; those who mourn, as if they did not; those who are happy, as if they were not; those who buy something, as if it were not theirs to keep; those who use the things of the world, as if not engrossed in them. For this world in its present form is passing away. I would like you to be free from concern. An un-married man is concerned about the Lord's affairs—how he can please the Lord. But a married man is concerned about the affairs of this world—how he can please his wife— and his interests are divided. An unmarried woman or virgin is concerned about the Lord's affairs: Her aim is to be devoted to the Lord in both body and spirit. But a married woman is concerned about the affairs of this world—how she can please her husband. I am saying this for your own good, not to restrict you, but that you may live in a right way in undivided devotion to the Lord. If anyone thinks he is acting improperly toward the virgin he is engaged to, and if she is getting along in years and he feels he ought to marry, he should do as he wants. He is not sinning. They should get married. But the man who has settled the matter in his own mind, who is under no compulsion but has control over his own will, and who has made up his mind not to marry the virgin—this man also does the right thing. So then, he who marries the virgin does right, but he who does not marry her does even better. A woman is bound to her husband as long as he lives. But if her husband dies, she is free to marry anyone she wishes, but he must belong to the Lord. In my judgment, she is happier if she stays as she is—and I think that I too have the Spirit of God."

Paul gives some very helpful advice here and to sum it all up in a nutshell he is saying that it is nothing wrong with being married and there is nothing wrong with be-ing single. He believes that it is better to be single because you can devote all of your time toward the work of God and this should be our aim as singles. However, Paul does say that the single person has to "settle the matter in their own mind, be under no compulsion, and have control over his own will." In other words, as singles we have to bring our bodies under the subjection of God and be free from compulsion. We shouldn't feel forced to live single but enjoy living single. Our mind has to be settled in the fact that whether we are single or not, we will choose to serve the Lord. You have to believe that singleness is a gift and you have to plan to use this gift to the best of your ability in order to bring about purpose.

Controlling the Desires of the Flesh

I believe this is probably one of the most important chapters where all singles want to know the answer to the question of how to control the desires of the flesh. Again, as I said earlier, we can love God with all of our hearts but we all have biological cravings and needs that still have to be managed. One of the powerful influences in my life was my Oversecr. Her name was Overseer Beatrice Marion. She used to always tell us that if you are highly sexual then you were highly anointed. I'm not sure how true it is but I did know this much, I was highly sexual and I know I'm highly anointed! Take note, I said I **"was"** highly sexual. Thank God for deliverance!

I hear people say often how they have been celibate for 10 or 12 years and this is wonderful. But how many of those years were you actually put in a situation where you were tempted. Let's be honest, I'm going to say something you may think is cruel but true. Some people have been celibate for that many years because there wasn't much opportunity for them to have someone. In plain terms nobody wanted them (smile). It's nothing wrong with being celibate all those years, this is an awesome accomplishment, but many are bombarded often with temptations to fall.

So when you hear from those who have been tempted often and chose to remain celibate regardless of the opposition, this is an even greater hope for the millions who struggle thinking they will never break through. If they can see someone who has battled in the flesh and overcome for 10 years then there is hope for them. I'm not saying that if you haven't been approached that this isn't a testimony because it is a great testimony. However, I am saying it is also a testimony of encouragement for those who were tempted, tried, sometimes gave in but with the power of God overcame! We all have a testimony from God that will help others but don't boast in your celibacy to the point where you want to make others feel inferior.

With me, I was able to understand why the enemy was attacking me in my flesh. It was to keep my vessel impure before God. I realized that the enemy attacks the body so that the Glory of God cannot flow through the body. God desires to use you as a vessel to pour his supernatural power through so that others may be set free. You have to have a clean and holy vessel. I knew my ministry would be a great deliverance ministry but I couldn't deliver others until I myself got delivered. I would not be able to see the miraculous happen now in my life if I had not purified my body and kept it holy before God. If your temple is unholy, God's glory will not reside in you. Your gifting may flow but his glory in you will not. If you remain operating in the flesh you will not receive God's best!

I don't know about you but I got tired of feeling empty, void and defeated because I couldn't get the victory over my flesh. However, I couldn't get past this point until I realized who I was in Christ and the power I had within me to overcome. I also had to learn practical steps in order to continue to overcome in my flesh.

I want to list below several things you can do in order to help prevent or stop the cravings of the flesh.

Control What Goes Through Your Eye Gates: You have to make sure that you are not allowing yourself to watch things on television that feed your sexual appetite. Such shows could be those that contain murder, romance, sex or sexual innuendos in them. All of these types of shows contribute to the lusting and cravings of the flesh. If you know you can't handle watching kissing on television without your flesh rising, then you need not watch it because you will be left alone with raging hormones.

Know your weaknesses in what you physically like in a partner because if you focus on those things you will again send your hormones raging. For example, a woman may like men the color of dark chocolate or a man may like blonde haired /blue eyed females. When you see a dark chocolate man or blonde hair blue eyed female walking by that looks pleasing to the eye, note that it's okay to look but not to daze.

What is dazing? According to the Webster dictionary; dazing means to look steadily and intently as with great curiosity, interest, pleasure, or wonder. When you are looking so intently that you begin receiving pleasure, you can leave an imprint on your soul that may later lead to raging hormones. Remember that dazing leads to craving!

Control What Goes Through Your Ear Gates: Make sure you are controlling what comes through your ears. If you cannot handle listening to love music without it making you reflect back on one of your past relationships then you need not listen to it. There are many songs out there that we all can reminisce on concerning past loves. I can think of many 80's songs that I use to love to listen to as a teenager concerning love and sex. My friends and I would sing those songs all day long. However, this can lead to adding fuel to the fire when it comes to fleshly desires. I just can't afford to listen to those types of songs now in my Christian walk. When you listen to music that feeds the flesh, eventually you are going to want to feed the flesh. If your favorite song as a single is "Let's get it on", then you may want to find another song or you will be getting it on! This may seem like common since but needs to be addressed in this book. I have made a choice that I will refuse to listen to any songs that feed the desires of my flesh! There is even some Christian music that has beats in them that can provoke the flesh so stay away from those as well.

As singles, you cannot afford to listen to sexual jokes or information about your friend's sex life. As a single person, most of my friends are married and I try not to make a habit of listening to what goes on in their sex life. If the conversation is brought up then I kindly ask them to change the subject because I can't afford to battle in my flesh when I'm alone. Remember, they have someone to release their sexual tension to. As singles living by God's standards we don't have a mate to release our sexual tension with. During this time of singleness in our life we can only release them to God.

Avoid Familiar Spirits from Past Lust Encounters: Once you have had a sexual encounter with someone and you have been set free from that soul-tie, you have to make sure you don't end up in the same situation God delivered you from. You will be able to do this by recognizing the symptoms that led you to the first encounter in order to help you avoid another encounter. For example, if you were in a relationship with a married person and God has delivered you from that area then you have to make sure you stay free of that. This means that when you see a married person who seems to catch your eye and "pull on your flesh" then you need to flee. If you feel something deep down in your soul that attracts you to that individual then you need to flee. God may have delivered you but Satan will often try to tempt you to see if you have been truly delivered.

Divorce yourself from Spirit Marriages: This can be a very controversial subject but to me it is a subject that needs to be dealt with and this is spirit marriages. Spirit marriages can be formed through curses, inheritance, perverseness, or any sexual relationship. They can enter through petting, kissing, flirting, lustful thoughts, sexual imaginations, or sexual idolatry. All of these things can open the door for spirit husbands and wives to enter into your life. When one has sexual relationships outside of what God's word commands, this often leads to spirit marriages.

I can remember being in prayer with a minister some time ago and he began to discuss the issue of spirit marriages. He began to say how singles needed to make sure that they were free from spirit marriages. He also began to say how many are bound and unable to get married because of these spirits. After that conversation I began to go before God in prayer and ask God to reveal to me any spirit marriages I may have had so that I could be delivered. To my surprise, God showed me 3 wedding bands on my ring finger. When I asked him about these bands he showed me three people that I had connected to in the spirit and never divorced. These came in through intimate encounters with 3 different individuals. So, I had to divorce and renounce these marriages in the spirit and confess my allegiance to God and my marriage to him alone.

Spirit marriages have also been called spirit husband and spirit wives known as incubus and succubus. The incubus spirit is an evil male spirit who sleeps with women in their sleep and the succubus spirit is an evil female spirit that comes to sleep with men at night. These spirits attack individuals while they are asleep and cause the individual to have orgasms while sleeping. These spirits not only attack singles but have also been known to attack individuals in marriages which often lead to adultery and divorce. If you have had this attack in your sleep before then you need to divorce this spirit. The spirit often attempts to hold you down in your sleep so that you are unable to speak or move.

If you desire to be free from this ask the Lord to reveal to you who, what, when and where it came in and then divorce these spirits. Once he has shown it to you, pray the prayer below.

Pray this prayer:

Father God in the name of Jesus, I repent from all sexual sins I have committed that have opened me up to marriage in the spiritual world. I recognize that a door has been opened in my life for this spirit marriage and I renounce it in Jesus name. Whether I was joined in marriage because of sexual perversion, adultery, fornication, immorality, uncleanness, idolatry, lust, rebellion or sexual addictions, I divorce my spirit mate now in Jesus' name.

I renounce every marriage covenant made between me and the spirit spouse or spouses. I also command all spirits that have entered or are hiding in my sexual organs to come out of my body in Jesus' name. I divorce every spirit spouse now in Jesus' name.

Father I thank you that as I sleep at night that you have put a wall of fire around me and have covered me from every incubus and succubus attack at night. Proverbs 3:24 says, When thou liest down, thou shalt not be afraid: yea, thou shalt lie down, and thy sleep shall be sweet. So I thank you for sweet sleep. The enemy will no longer come at night and sow tares in my life. Arrows of the night assigned against my life, back fire in Jesus' name. Every power holding me down in iniquity, break off in Jesus name! Blood of Jesus, arise in your power and envelope my body in Jesus' name!

Once you have prayed this prayer in faith believe that he has freed you and don't open the door back up to seven worse spirits than before through sexual immorality. Everyday renew your mind, commitment and relationship to God. Men always keep the Lord Jesus as head over your life as father and protector against lustful demons waging against your life and your destiny. Draw nigh to God every day of your life so that he draws nigh to you. This is the only way to stay free. Flee fornication as the scripture has commanded.

Remember The Anointing Attracts: Any sincere Christian individual wants to be with someone that compliments them and brings good companionship. However, we have to be careful that we don't allow a person's anointing to outweigh God's will for our individual lives.

The Greek word for anointing is "Chrisma." The word Chrisma means the special endowment of the Holy Spirit.

When a person operates in the anointing they are operating outside of their natural flesh and have tapped into the supernatural realm of God. They have transitioned themselves into a place of where the Holy Spirit resides and this is a place of the divine or supernatural. Everyone is attracted to the divine or supernatural whether they realize it or not. They are attracted to this because human nature gravitates to that which is beyond themselves. God placed this gravitation toward the supernatural as a means to connect with him not to fleshly desires.

The reason I have emphasized this is because we have to understand that **the flesh can never appease the anointing**. So many times individuals have tried to seize the anointing through fleshly means. When I say through fleshly means, I mean often times through sex. When one is attracted to the anointing it ignites all parts of your being. When a person is anointed by the Holy Spirit and operating in that anointing; their whole body, soul and spirit is involved with moving in the things of God. Their body houses this active anointing and becomes a magnet attracting everything it comes in contact with. This is why preachers, church leaders, and Christians often times fall into fornication. This happens because the person tries to satisfy the anointing with the flesh not realizing that the anointing can only be satisfied with holiness.

John 3:6 says, *"Flesh gives birth to flesh, but the Spirit gives birth to spirit."*

The flesh is separate and the spirit is separate. We can't appease the Holy Spirit with the flesh!

I would like to give you an example of this. Let's say you are in a room filled with anointed people and you are a

Christian single. There are many anointed people in the room. Some are married, some are not, some are dating others, some are not, and some are to be married to others but none are to be married to you in that particular room. You have to recognize that although you are anointed and attracted to the anointing of many in the room, none of these individuals are ordained for you. Therefore, when your flesh starts to pull towards any of those people in the room, you have to renounce those feelings and dismiss them immediately because to have those feelings are fleshly and false. But if you go ahead with one of the individuals in the room and act upon these fleshly feelings, you have moved into an illegal realm that would only yield disappointment. This is even true with non-Christian singles. People are often operating in the realm of the flesh and continue to yield disappointment and dissatisfaction.

There is something that we have to understand about the anointing. The anointing recognizes the anointing but the body recognizes the body. We have to understand that the body doesn't know how to handle the anointing and we have to train it to be submissive to the Holy Spirit. This means doing as Paul says and keep our body under subjection of the Holy Spirit. He says this in 1 Corinthians 9:27,

"But I keep under my body, and bring it into subjection: lest that by any means, when I have preached to others, I myself should be a castaway." If we look at the Amplified version of the bible we see that it says, *"But [like a boxer] I buffet my body [handle it roughly, discipline it by hardships] and subdue it, for fear that after proclaiming to others the Gospel and things pertaining to it, I myself should become unfit [not stand the test, be unapproved and rejected as a counterfeit]."*

We have a duty to keep our flesh under control regardless of how we feel and what our false desires may be. The false may feel right but will get us into trouble.

The bible also tells us in 1 Corinthians 6:18, *"Flee fornication. Every sin that a man doeth is without the body; but he that committeth fornication sinneth against his own body." Therefore, if the temptation comes, flee."*

It is funny but true; your past will always try to find you but don't let it in.

Jesus said in Luke 11: 24-26, *"When the unclean spirit is gone out of a man, he walketh through dry places, seeking rest; and finding none, he saith, I will return unto my house whence I came out. And when he cometh, he findeth it swept and garnished. Then goeth he, and taketh to him seven other spirits more wicked than himself; and they enter in, and dwell there: and the last state of that man is worse than the first."*

You can't afford to fall back into a worse state. Keep yourself clean through prayer and meditation upon the word.

You also need to get rid of any items from the past that involved your previous sex partners. If they gave you a diamond watch, jewelry, movies, cologne, clothes, pictures, etc. Get rid of them! You don't need anything keeping your soul tied to theirs! If you find that there is a struggle to get rid of all of these items then you are at risk for a relapse!

Channel Your Emotions: The online dictionary defines the word channel as meaning "a course into which something may be directed. It is a route through which anything passes or progresses." When you find that biologically your hormones are raging, you do not need to focus on those feelings but channel those feelings. I would probably consider this the number one thing to do in order to control the desires of your flesh.

There are several things you can do in order to channel your feelings. You can exercise, pray about something separate from what you are feeling, or do anything else that will take your mind off of what you are feeling. Make sure that whatever you choose, it is constructive for you and not destructive.

You can also mentally see yourself releasing your feelings to God. This has helped me a lot. I will be honest with God and tell him, "Lord....my hormones are really acting up now and I need you to take my feelings upon you." Understand that sexual feelings will never permanently go away because this is a part of our genetic makeup. However, you can learn how to cast your feelings upon God until when or if your mate comes. I say this because everyone will not marry and that's okay. If there is a strong desire in you to be married then God can honor that desire but there are those who are truly satisfied with being single.

When I cast my feelings upon the Lord, I literally see myself placing my feelings upon him and he takes it away. You have to envision in your mind God taking those emotions upon him. This is scriptural. In 1 Peter 5:7 it says, *"Casting all your care upon him; for he careth for you."* As you see yourself casting your feelings onto God, allow him to take them upon himself and the emotions will leave. You have to see a mental picture of God in your mind and see yourself releasing those feelings to him until the pressures of those feelings have gone. Many times I have done this and it works. The key is to be consistent with this. We can't cast our cares on God when we feel like it. We have to cast our feelings upon him each time we begin to feel this way and we can trust that he will literally take our feelings upon him.

Remember, Proverbs 23:7 says, *"For as he thinketh in his heart, so is he."* Whatever we think about is what we will experience in our life. If we think about God's presence we will experience his presence. If we think about God's promises in the word of God, we will experience the promises of the word of God in our lives. The same is true when it comes to our emotions. If we think about sexual feelings then our body will react to those feelings. We will then begin to experience the cravings of sex. In the same manner, if we think about casting our emotions upon God then he will take on our emotions and we will experience peace.

If we don't learn how to be consistent in channeling our emotions onto God, we will continue to go through struggles in the flesh. Often people prefer to think about what they are feeling in their emotions and it makes the struggle worse. Decide to choose to cast your burdens upon the Lord. It takes discipline and help of the Holy Spirit but you can do it.

If you are a minister, recognize that nine times out of ten, after you have preached your longing for sex may increase because you are on a spiritual high. Satan often attacks us at this most vulnerable time. Your body doesn't know how to react to the spiritual realm. Therefore, after preaching surround yourself with an atmosphere that is conducive for you when coming down out of the spirit realm. Turn to him through communion and prayer with him. Feed yourself those things that are positive for your spirit.

It may be surrounding yourself with the love of family, friends, children, a wholesome movie, a mini-trip or etc. Whatever it takes to keep you pure before the Lord after ministering then do it.

Recognize that after you preach, you don't have a mate to go home to and your option is not to settle for temporary sex and fulfillment. If you don't accept this, you will always be stunted in your growth in God. You will always look for fulfillment in others. Recognize that no person will be able to take the place of God when it comes to filling you back up after you minister as a single minster.

Take Care of Your Health: Taking care of your health is very important because it contributes in some ways to your hormonal changes. Make sure you eat right. It is also important to make sure that you get regular checkups to make sure that everything is functioning properly inside your body. If there is a chemical imbalance in your body then you could begin to have emotional and physical cravings. Check your blood sugar and exercise to relieve stress. If you are stressed for long periods of time then you are more likely to give into temptations because you are vulnerable. Get rest!!!!

These practical steps will help you overcome the lusts and desires of the flesh. If we learn how to counteract Satan and his schemes through these steps we can move further in God. We have to recognize that Satan wants to distract us through our emotions and other circumstances. Learn your weakness and pitfalls in which Satan has caused you to fall in the past so that you are able to be victorious. Learn to stay focused long enough to channel your emotions toward God-given abilities and then you will be fulfilled.

As singles, we have to break the cycle and let God fill us to the fullness with his presence and power. It is okay to have companions such as friends, family, mentors, spiritual parents, food, hobbies and etc. However, recognize that these cannot quench the hunger in your soul like God can.

Reflection Questions

1. Out of the six ways given in this chapter on how to control the flesh, which three do you feel you need to work on the most and why?

2. What is the one thing you will do differently when it comes to controlling the appetites of the flesh?

Chapter 8

I'll Have A Virgin Daiquiri Please!

Especially for Virgins

I want to dedicate this chapter to my God daughter in college studying with plans for law school, my virgin sisters in Christ and all of the virgins in the world. You have been blessed with a priceless gift and it is my prayer that you cherish this gift until you meet the right person.

One of my favorite past times to relax is to have a good meal. Every time I go to a restaurant I love to order special virgin drinks. My friends and family know that the majority of the times after my meal, I will always order a special virgin drink. If I choose no drink I can still enjoy the luxuries that virgin drinks bring. So usually when I go out to a restaurant I will ask for a virgin daiquiri because it has all of the ingredients of a strawberry daiquiri but without the alcohol.

I remember being out on a date with a boyfriend and when we went out to eat, I ordered a virgin daiquiri. When my order came back I noticed that it was not virgin and I told my boyfriend. He was like, "So what…. it's okay." Well because I was a Christian and trying to live for the Lord drinking was a problem for me. He was a Christian as well but it wasn't a problem for him. However, I sent the drink back and asked for a virgin. If you drink alcohol that is between you and your God but I had to follow my convictions.

A regular strawberry daiquiri includes white rum which is considered an ethanol or better known as alcohol. It is the chemical conversion of sugar into ethanol. Ethanol is considered flammable and is also considered a psychoactive drug. A psychoactive drug affects the brain resulting in changes of your perception, your mood, your consciousness, and your behavior. This is why alcoholic drinks are often times called "spirits." You can often become intoxicated when you consume more than your individual tolerance for alcohol. Your mental and physical abilities become impaired.

In some way, this is how I see all of those who have held out and not given in to the temptations of sex outside of marriage. You have chosen to wait on God and not mix that which is sweet with that which can burn you! You have decided not to allow yourself to be opened up to spirits that will affect your perception, your mood, your consciousness and your behavior. Sex will change you and if you are not careful it will also intoxicate you.

As I mentioned earlier, I remember the times of working with young women and men who were always more than likely to have had sex. These youth were middle school age and higher and there were even some elementary school kids who were sexually active. A good number of them were attending church and considered themselves Christians. At times, I would often feel sad because of this. I had begun to think that the odds were against virginity because I had seen so much sexual activity going on among the youth.

However, I remember one year I came across a young lady who was graduating from high school that used to be in my teen pregnancy prevention program. She was graduating from high school and had mentioned how she was still a virgin and was proud. I couldn't believe it! I was shocked. I had become so numb and disheartened by the fact that so many teens were having sex that I forgot about those who weren't. This opened my heart up again to see that there are those who are still choosing to wait to have sex. On my job, I had seen the statistics on how there were teens that hose to remain abstinent but among the youth I encountered on a day to day basis, it was far and few.

Then something happened that sparked hope back into me. I was working at a middle school during my last year as a teen pregnancy prevention specialist. We had conducted a pre-test concerning youth risk behaviors and I was pleasantly surprised to find out that many were still virgins both boys and girls. I believe that God was using this as an encouragement to me.

God even went further to show me encouragement in the area of those Christian youth who have chosen to wait to have sex. I was blessed to meet a beautiful young lady who told me that she is still a virgin and is waiting on God. She is currently in college as an English major in Alabama and is still holding out for God.

I also remembered facilitating a singles seminar on dealing with temptations, dating, sex, and waiting on God. During that meeting, what I didn't realize was that there was a virgin in attendance. She was not a teen but a young adult who had recently completed college. She is still holding on to her virginity with pride. Several women in the room just envied her and told her how they wish they could be a virgin again. She made a statement that tongue kissing would really be like sex for her. Boy was I amazed, it's sad but it is true. Why should we be amazed about standards that we as single Christians should have? It is because the truth of the matter is that there are many single Christians out there that are sexually active or have been sexually active at least once in their life time.

I remember this same young lady sharing at another singles seminar how her mother taught her that her virginity was a gift and that she shouldn't just give it up to any and everybody. So this is what she chose to do and she made her choice wisely. She mentioned that she is tempted but because she doesn't know what it is like, the temptation doesn't bother her as much. Through her testimony, I can truly say that God is a keeper!

Some of you may be saying that's good for her but I didn't have a choice because my virginity was taken away through rape or molestation. This was also the case for me. My virginity was taken away from me at a young age but it wasn't my fault and it's not your fault. However, we do have a choice now to remain celibate. We have to be delivered from that demon and continue to fight off the spirit of promiscuity by leaning on God. We are also able to minister to those who have come through the same situation and encourage them to keep pressing forward. We can use the gift of celibacy in order to show that God is the greatest restorer and keeper if we want to be kept.

I just want to say to every virgin out there to wear your virginity with pride and dignity. In my opinion, when it comes to sex outside of marriage, as virgins, you have escaped the complications it brings. It is God that has given you the strength to hold out and you have been given a great gift. Don't take your gift lightly because many wish they could turn back the hands of time to become a virgin again.

However, I do want to say try to never use your virginity in haughtiness or as an idol. Don't use your gift of virginity to condemn others but use it to encourage others. Take this gift and us it in humility. Use it to encourage all the young men and women who have been favored to continue their walk in their virginity. Show them that with all things God is able to keep them regardless of what the world is doing.

Reflection Questions

1. If your virginity was taken from you against your will, how have you taken the steps to be healed from this unfortunate situation? What steps were taken and how do you know you are healed?

2. How will you use your virginity or celibacy for the glory of God?

3. Can you think of one Adult that you know personally that is single and still a virgin?

4. If you are not a virgin, are you celibate? If not, what can you personally do in order to live a life of celibacy and what is holding you back?

Chapter 9

Famous Singles

In the previous chapter, I mentioned how everyone will not get married and that is okay. Some people enjoy being single and don't desire to be married. However, there are other people that are single due to life circumstances and not by choice.

God gives grace to each person according to the season they are walking through in life. He will strengthen you in your singleness. You can live a joyous, productive, and successful life as a single person but it is your choice. When we realize that we are single, not according to the world's standards but according to God standards, then we will maximize the potential God has given us. We will discuss some of these ways later on but I first want to give you a list of some very successful singles during previous times, our time period and during bible times.

From times past and present, singles have become successful citizens in our society. Some of these are:

Wilhelm Eduard Weber: He was a professor of Theology at the University of Wittenberg and published the famous paper, which contained experimental investigations of water and sound waves. He later became a professor of physics and other scientists developed theories from his ideas.

Sir Isaac Newton: He was an English Scientist known throughout the world as the father of modern science. He was a theologian, mathematician, physicist, astronomer, and natural philosopher.

Jane Austin: She was the daughter of an English clergyman whose novels often had religious implications in them. She became a famous English writer that authored 2 novels that were both made into Hollywood movies. These were Sense and Sensibility and Pride and Prejudice.

James Buchanan, Jr. He was the only president that never married. He was the 15th president.

Susan B. Anthony: She was a school teacher involved in the temperance and abolitionist movements.

Andrew Jackson: He was a widow for 19 years before he was elected as the third president.

Dr. Condoleeza Rice: She was the U.S. Secretary of State and the first African-American woman to hold that Cabinet post. She also previously served as National Security Advisor.

George Washington Carver: He was a professor, researcher, and American agricultural chemist who devoted his time to southern agriculture. He was able to look at many different ways in which he and other farmers could improve economic situations. He developed 300 derivative products from peanuts such as coffee, milk and cheese and 118 derivative products from sweet potatoes such as molasses and rubber ink.

These are only a few of the countless singles that decided to pursue their purpose regardless of their singleness. They saw their singleness as a gift and used it in order to help others. We can also see these examples of singles mentioned in the bible.

Here are some of the singles mentioned in the bible that did extraordinary works for the kingdom of God.

Old Testament Singles

Miriam: She was the oldest sister of Moses and was a prophetess. She ended up being the first songstress in the bible to lead the first choir in the bible.

Elijah: He was the most influential prophet of Israel. Elijah was one of the few who went to heaven without even physically dying. He worked many miracles of God and was a national prophet.

Elisha: He was a major prophet in the bible who was able to mingle with ordinary people but exhibit God's extraordinary power in the earth. He was able to do many miracles, signs and wonders that often resembled those of Jesus.

Jeremiah: Although he wasn't successful according to the world standards and underwent much harsh treatment, he received supernatural strength to endure rejection from an entire southern kingdom of Judah and still remained faithful to God. He was a major prophet who prophesied the 70 year captivity of Babylon and was able to see it. He was specifically chosen by God in his mother's womb and God chose him to be a spokesman to the world.

Daniel: He was a prophet whom God gave the supernatural ability to interpret dreams and visions. He was an advisor to two Babylonian kings and two Medo-Persian kings. His prophetic gifting allowed him to give a preview of God's redemption and has been called the key to all biblical prophecy.

New Testament Singles

Anna: She was a prophetess who was married for 7 years and then became a widow for 84 years. She served God with fasting and prayers day and night.

Jesus Christ: He should be considered the #1 role model for singles and all people. As a single person, he brought salvation to all mankind and he is the greatest miracle worker of all times. He knew his purpose and didn't' care what others thought about him. He let nothing stop him from reaching his destiny. He defeated Satan on our behalf once and for all. There is nothing else that really needs to be said. He is the son of God who has all power and is considered equal to God. He is our savior and Lord!

Mary Magdalene: Although she had a horrible past that allowed her to be possessed with 7 demons, Jesus was able to deliver her. She then became one of Jesus' most faithful followers, going with him all the way to the cross. She was the first to witness the resurrection of Jesus and to report it to the apostles.

Apostle John: He was the author of five books and letters of the New Testament which includes the book of Revelations.

Apostle Paul: He was a person gifted and anointed for singleness! He writes about the importance of singleness in I Corinthians 7:7-8 as I previously discussed. He considered singleness as a gift and we who are single should as well.

He also wrote half of the New Testament's 27 books and letters and became the most successful missionary and church planter. He was the first to take the gospel to the world and make it a faith all could receive by taking the gospel to the Gentiles.

Lydia: She was a one of the most wealthy and successful business women in Europe who sold purple dye. She accommodated Paul and his missionary team in the city of Philippi. Lydia became a charter member of the Philippians church. She was the first Christian Convert in Europe and her home became the first meeting place of Christians in Europe. (Acts 16)

Philip's daughters: They were four unmarried daughters of the evangelist Philip. They were prophetesses of God who were great teachers of God's word.

So we are able to see that there we many people who were single in the bible that enjoyed their singleness. They understood that they had a purpose in life and didn't allow their singleness to hinder them from reaching their full potential in God.

The world is waiting for your contribution to be added to the singles hall of fame. You don't have to sulk in pity and loneliness because of your singleness. Make this your aim and goal to make a lasting impression on society as a single person.

Reflection Questions

1. What will you do in order to be recognized as a successful single person?

2. What have you contributed to society as a single person?

3. You may eventually end up married but what will be your contribution to life before that time?

Chapter 10

Holding Out For God's Perfect Will

As you are waiting with God and holding out for God's perfect will in your life, you have to learn how to pray, fast, and trust God. I know you have heard this many times before but it is true. While you are waiting, you need to give yourself to all of the gifts and talents you have yet to utilize. What is it that you love to do? Do you like to dance, sing, paint, swim, counsel, or write? Whatever it is you love to do, take it and do it with all of your might for the glory of God.

For example, I love to travel so every year I make a decision to travel to a different state that I've never been before. This gives me a chance to enjoy God's creation and enjoy my freedom while I am single. Also, I love to write, so when I get lonely sometimes I write. When the desire is there to be with someone and I feel the spirit of loneliness trying to creep in, I will pick up a pen and start writing. This really helps me to release positive energy. However, traveling or writing may not be your thing but find out what works for **you** that will push **you** toward **your** destiny and enrich **your** life. Try a new hobby and do other things to enrich you cultural environment.

There are going to be times when your hormones are raging and the spirit of loneliness will try to lay heavy on your mind and heart. However, you have to make a conscious decision to wait those feelings out and not give in to the flesh. There were days when my hormones would rage and I would try to do everything to ward off those feelings and it seemed nothing would work. So I would just sit and wait. I've had to learn to discipline my emotions and feelings and just wait in God. I would just talk to God and ask him to help me because I've been through giving into the flesh. All giving into the flesh does is leave me lonely afterwards. I may have been physically filled for that period of time, but after that time is over I was left empty. So I just wait it out in God. I may even go to sleep with raging hormones but by the next day when I wake up I am fine. Psalm 30:5 says, "...*weeping may endure for a night, but joy cometh in the morning.*" Some days are tougher than others but if we are determined to wait on God's will for our lives then we will do whatever it takes to wait. God will help us if we want to be helped and he will strengthen us if we desire to be strengthened.

Society trains us to gratify the flesh and feed it what it needs. However, we have to be in control of our flesh and tell it we are in control. Of course, I didn't always keep my flesh in control but through trusting in God, he has helped me.

THE GREATER ONE LIVE'S IN US

The greater one lives within us but we have to let him live and be the greater one in us. We are going to have to make choices that keep us free from loneliness, self-destructing behaviors, and sin.

When you recognize that there is something inside of you bigger than what is on the outside of you, you will want to nurture what is on the inside. There is greatness inside of you and potential that you haven't tapped into and it is time to allow that potential to come forward. Make a decision to no longer let your emotions control your destiny.

One of the greatest challenges as singles will be to allow the inner to transform the outer. We have to let the greater one within us override the outer part of us. Will you risk it all to follow after the gift of God within you and rise above status quo? Everyone is able to cater to the fleshly desires of the body, give into the feelings of loneliness, and sulk about what they don't have. However, it takes power in God and belief in yourself to know that you can rise above status quo. It is time to look in the mirror at yourself and see what God see's in you. You are more than what your emotions, will, body, and fleshly mind dictate to you. I have written a poem that I desire to share with you. You have to take a look at yourself in the mirror and see what God sees in you.

"WHEN I LOOK IN THE MIRROR"

When I look in the mirror, what do I see?
Carmel lips, wavy hair, and narrow brown feet.
When I look in the mirror, it glares back at me...
Beholding a size 12 instead of a size 3.

When I look in the mirror, what do I see?
The eyes of my soul peering out from the deep.
When I look in the mirror, it glares back at me...
With fear, rejection, and insecurity.
When I look in the mirror, what do I see?
O, So many things I wish I could be.
When I look in the mirror it glares back at me...
With a mind that's filled with curiosity.
When I look in the mirror, what do I see?
A butterfly changing into a new me.
When I look in the mirror, it glares back at me...
From the eyes of God's heart, with blissful glee.
When I look in the mirror, what do I see?
His grace, his love, and unmerited mercy.
When I look in the mirror, it glares back at me...
Beholding a bold, courageous and confident me.
When I look in the mirror, what do I see?
I'm winning hard, strong, and victoriously.

This is a poem that God gave me to encourage me. As singles we have to see ourselves as God sees us and that is victorious and made in his image. The greater one shines through us in all of our gifts, talents, and spiritual achievements. Today is the day to allow him to shine forth for his glory. We are more than our mind, will and emotions. We are spiritual beings with the supernatural ability to accomplish all our hearts desire. We are to be ambassadors for his Kingdom and purposed to be a shining light for others. As singles, we have the gifting and ability to touch others with our time, talent, strength, and inner beauty.

The greater one is yearning to come out and bless those around you so start today. Make a decision today not to allow anything to hinder you from greatness.

Conclusion

Position Yourself

You have to be determined to position yourself in a place where you are able to reach your hearts' desire outside of desiring a mate. Do other things that help you to reach your inward desires and goals. As I said earlier, I loved to travel so I did that. Also, I desired to meet different people who have accomplished much in their lives so I set goals in order to meet them. Many of these things helped me to fulfill the inner longing I had within my being and you can do the same.

When the spirit of loneliness would try to come into my life, I would put myself in a position where I was able to meditate on the things that God has allowed me to accomplish. I also prayed for direction on how to carry out other desires I wanted to achieve and I would set out to accomplish those desires.

If our sole focus is to truly love God, then he will bless us with our hearts desire. I remember telling God that there was a particular celebrity I desired to meet and through prayer he revealed to me that I would meet them. I held on to that promise and in December 11, 2009, he opened that door for me. God has answered my personal heart's desire and it has pushed me with such a hunger and desire today that I am now obtaining things that I would have never thought to obtain. I believe you will be doing the same and more!

I am here to motivate you. Push yourself, reposition yourself, break the mold and break the door today to walk out of a lonely heart into a fulfilled heart. You have to realize that having a mate would be nice but you have to be comfortable enough with yourself to say it won't be the end of the world if he or she never comes. You realize that it just means that God has great need of you as a single person to fulfill a great destiny. Your singleness is an opportunity and blessing to complete your destiny.

You may crave companionship within a mate but if you don't have that companionship right now it's because God wants you to fulfill other longings within your heart. Some of you may say, "I don't have any other longing besides a mate." Then you need to recognize this as a sign that you lack a longing for God because remember, God is the one who fills the void in our heart not man. Man can be used to help this longing but God is the ultimate source to fill the longing. As we seek the Lord he births in us other longings and dreams to fulfill until our mate comes. We have to reposition ourselves to be so in tune with God that we know he loves us and has our best interest at heart. When we tap into God he shows us our true longing which is to fulfill his will in our lives. He will give us wisdom on how to fulfill this God given longing and then the loneliness we once felt will turn into a life full of fulfillment, health, and joy. When we position ourselves to have a healthy longing for God we recognize that loneliness is only a state of mind. Our thought and heart patterns begin to shift. We begin pressing towards our inward longings that cause us to succeed and then the loneliness we once felt begins to diminish.

I am rooting for you and know that you have already accomplished your maximum potential in God. You no longer have a lonely heart but you are able to spread forth your wings and fly. As I finish this book, I would like to leave you with one final poem of encouragement for you that I have written.

"Fly"

Why is it hard at times to push where I know I need to go?
Towards a purpose deep within that's begging out to grow
Self-deceptions, insecurities, lack of faith and pain
Causes me to mourn with agony, frustration and disdain
Fly is what I tell myself when my inner heart is blue
Fly is what I tell myself when I don't know what to do
As time continues to tick and destiny continues to delay
As unattended goals are left to finish for another day
Fly is what I tell myself when destiny is in demand
Fly is what I tell myself towards God's unchanging hand

Today I want to encourage you to fly to your highest potential. This has always been my prayer to God. My desire has always been to fly as high as I can in him. I desire to leave this earth with all the potential inside of me fulfilled. I want to leave empty - completing my task and finishing the race. I pray the same for you today my friend. Fly as high as you can into God's unchanging hand. He will direct you out of every lonely place into a place that is rich with fulfillment. He will allow you to "suck honey out of the rock and wash your steps with butter."

I want to leave you with one of my favorite scriptures in Numbers 6:24-26 which says, *"May the LORD bless you and protect you. May the LORD smile on you and be gracious to you. May the LORD show you his favor and give you his peace."*

Reflection Questions

1. What gifts and talents do you have to use for the glory of God and how will you start?

2. What will be the biggest challenge in you repositioning yourself to be in tune with God so that you are able tap into fulfilling your God given longing?

3. How will you plan to overcome this challenge?

References

Merriam-Webster's Dictionary
Eleventh Edition, First Printing 2003
Springfield, Massachusetts, U.S.A

Study First to Link TV Sex to Real Teen Pregnancies
By Rob Stein
Washington Post Staff Writer
Monday, November 3, 2008
http://www.washingtonpost.com/wp-dyn/content/article/2008/11/02/AR2008110202592.html?sid=ST2008110300038
(Public Domain)

Maslow's Hierarchy of Needs
Wikipedia Free Online Encyclopedia
en.wikipedia.org/wiki/**Maslow's_hierarchy_of_needs**
(Public Domain)

Biblegateway
King James Version of the Bible
NIV Version of the Bible
biblegateway.com
(Public Domain)

Dictionary
Dictionary.com
(Public Domain)

www.ingramcontent.com/pod-product-compliance
Lightning Source LLC
Chambersburg PA
CBHW061734020426
42331CB00006B/1236